IMMIGRANT
Children

IMMIGRANT
Children

Sylvia Whitman

Carolrhoda Books, Inc./Minneapolis

To Majida, our little deglat el-noor

Page one: A young Italian immigrant struggles to carry a box in 1926.
Page two: Immigrant children found new opportunities in America. These children play at their New York City elementary school in the early 1900s.
Opposite page: Norwegian immigrants on a ship bound for America in 1904

Carolrhoda Books, Inc.
A Division of Lerner Publishing Group
241 First Avenue North
Minneapolis, MN 55401 U.S.A.

Website address: www.lernerbooks.com

LIBRARY OF CONGRESS CATALOGING-IN-PUBLICATION DATA

Whitman, Sylvia, 1961–
    Immigrant children / Sylvia Whitman.
        p.   cm. — (Picture the American past)
    Includes bibliographical references and index.
    Summary: Describes the flood of immigration into the United States in the late nineteenth and early twentieth centuries, focusing on the experiences of the youngest immigrants, both on their journeys and in their new country.
    ISBN 1-57505-395-0
    1.Children of immigrants—United States—History—Juvenile literature. [1. Immigrants. 2. United States—Emigration and immigration.] I. Title. II. Series.
JV6600.W55 2000
305.23'0973'09034—dc21   99-29294

Manufactured in the United States of America
1 2 3 4 5 6 – JR – 05 04 03 02 01 00

CONTENTS

Above: A mother and children arrive at the immigration station on Ellis Island in about 1910.
Opposite page: From Ellis Island, immigrant children view New York City across the harbor.

Through the Golden Door

Give me your tired, your poor,
Your huddled masses yearning to breathe free. . . .
I lift up my lamp beside the golden door!
—from an 1883 poem by Emma Lazarus,
on the Statue of Liberty

Waves of people washed onto the shores of the United States. The country was growing and needed workers. Between the 1820s and the 1920s, more than 35 million immigrants moved here from all over the world.

Immigrants arrived hungry, bruised, and hopeful. Some men traveled alone. They planned to work for a while and then return home. Others brought wives and children or sent for them later. Everyone was looking for a better life.

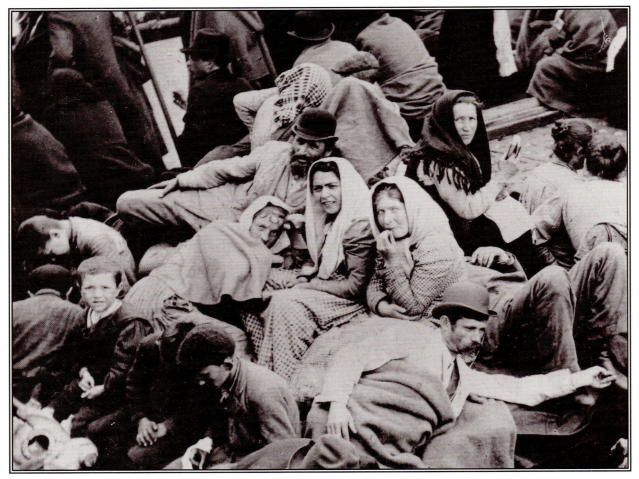

Passengers on the deck of a ship from Europe heading for New York in 1902

Most immigrants steamed toward the unknown on jam-packed ships. A woman who left Russia at age eight said, "Going to America then was almost like going to the moon."

New York. Two young immigrants from Scandinavia leave a ferryboat.

At first, the government didn't keep track of immigrants. Then it set up stations at ports. By the 1890s, the busiest station was Ellis Island, off New York City.

Inspectors boarded ships and checked rich passengers. The rich could leave when the ship docked. The poor had to take ferryboats to Ellis Island.

New York. People fill the main hall at Ellis Island in about 1912.

The main building at Ellis Island looked like a redbrick palace. Scared and excited, immigrants lined up outside. They wore tags from their ships. Many had put on their best clothes. They wanted to pass inspection.

Immigrants left their bags in the hall. As doctors watched, everyone climbed the stairs to a huge, open room.

New York. While other immigrants wait their turn, a young woman is examined by doctors on Ellis Island.

With chalk, doctors wrote letters on the clothes of anyone who seemed sick—*B* for back, *F* for face, *Sc* for scalp, *L* for lameness. They paid extra attention to the marked people.

Boys and girls with common diseases like measles were sent to the island hospital. Many immigrants didn't speak English. Often they didn't understand what was happening. Nurses tried to explain and make children feel better. The hospital warned loving nurses, "Do not kiss a patient."

Children who recovered rejoined their families. But the United States didn't accept people with serious health problems. They were sent back to their old homes.

New York. A mother and children, turned back by inspectors, wait to return to Europe.

New York. All immigrants were examined for trachoma, an eye disease.

Most people who came from Europe passed through Ellis Island. Most people who came from Asia passed through Angel Island, near San Francisco. At every station, immigrants dreaded the eye exam. Doctors looked for an infection that caused blindness.

The exam hurt. Doctors flipped each eyelid with a hook—the same kind ladies used to button their shoes and gloves. The hook may have spread germs because doctors didn't wash it. They just wiped it on a towel.

New York. Children wait in the main baggage room at Ellis Island.

Next, immigrants faced an inspector. He asked where immigrants were from and how much money they had. He wrote notes about their hometowns, families, and jobs. The United States wanted people who could take care of themselves. Helpers translated the many questions and answers.

Within a day, most families received a landing card. Then they could leave. A dozen railroad companies sold tickets on the island, although the trains left from the mainland. Many immigrants put on new tags so that conductors could help them get onto the right train and off in the right town.

Immigrants who failed inspection had to stay until a ship took them back overseas. They called Ellis the "Island of Tears."

Even women and children who passed inspection were not allowed to leave until a man from the family met them, or sent a letter or a ticket. They waited days, weeks, months, even years.

California. Chinese women and children wait on Angel Island near San Francisco. Angel Island was an immigration station from 1909 until 1949.

New York. In the dining hall on Ellis Island, the long benches were crammed, but the food was hot—and free. This room could seat 1,200 hungry immigrants.

Waiting families slept in dorms, in wire-mesh beds stacked like shelves. Immigrants ate in the dining hall. The food wasn't fancy, but there was plenty. Some boys and girls tasted ice cream for the first time. Twice a day, a man in a white uniform served mothers and children warm milk in paper cups.

New York. Children play in the sun on the rooftop garden and playground at Ellis Island around 1910.

Children played on swings, bikes, and a merry-go-round on a roof at Ellis Island. Everyone was wondering about America, across the water.

Lucky immigrants had relatives waiting at the "Kissing Gate." Families had been apart a long time. One Russian girl saw a "beautiful" man. She didn't know he was her father. "Later on I realized why he looked so familiar to me. He looked exactly like I did. . . . And I fell in love with him and he with me."

Above: Norwegian settlers relax in a field near Madison, Wisconsin, at mid-harvest in the late 1800s.
Opposite page: A widow and her 11 children pose at Ellis Island in 1908 before traveling on to Loretta, Minnesota.

Starting from Scratch

In America life is gold.
In America it's never dark.
In America there's lots of money.
In America the girl is happy.
  —Hungarian folk song, 1920s

Immigrants settled all over the United States. Since western land was cheap, many tried farming. After the Homestead Act was passed in 1862, native-born and immigrant settlers headed west to claim free land.

Newcomers liked to live near others who shared their language and religion. They traded recipes and talked about the old country. Used to cold weather, people from Sweden and Norway felt at home in the Midwest.

The United States became a quilt of immigrants. Following jobs, they settled in patches. French Canadians moved to New England, near mills that made cloth. The Chinese lived in the West, near railroad tracks they laid. Miners from Europe dug for coal in Pennsylvania.

Pennsylvania. Many young immigrants found work in coal mines in the late 1800s and early 1900s.

Most newcomers settled in cities. Immigrants helped make cities big and bustling. In New York, Boston, Chicago, Cleveland, and Detroit, immigrants and their children soon outnumbered the native born.

New York City. Immigrant neighborhoods, such as the Lower East Side, shown here in about 1898, were filled with people and activity.

San Francisco. Young and old immigrants in Chinatown

Even in cities, people from the same country stuck together. Many cities had a "Little Italy" or a "Chinatown." These neighborhoods were like tiny nations.

Immigrants started newspapers in their own languages. Some families opened food stores. Shoppers could buy German pretzels or Dutch coleslaw. The Irish filled Catholic churches in Boston while the Jews built temples in New York.

Neighborhoods were lively. Immigrants ran theaters, bars, restaurants, music groups, dance halls, and sports clubs.

Saint Paul, Minnesota. German immigrants believed that exercise was good for both boys and girls. Girls in an exercise club called a turnverein *pose in 1892.*

New York City. An Italian immigrant mother and her children crowd into a tiny apartment in 1910.

People fresh off the boat were nicknamed "greenhorns." They arrived with almost nothing.

The poor crowded into tiny apartments in tall buildings. Families often slept, cooked, and ate in one room. Even when the toilet in the hall worked, it stank. A nine-year-old girl who lived in a basement saw "rats as big as cats."

New York City. In some city apartments, mothers gave baths to children and did the laundry in the same sink.

It was hard to keep anything clean, but mothers tried. They washed clothes and children once a week.

Buildings were noisy, smelly, and dark—cold in winter, hot in summer. Flies buzzed around the waste that horses plopped and people slopped into the streets. To cool off, families sat—or slept—on the fire escape.

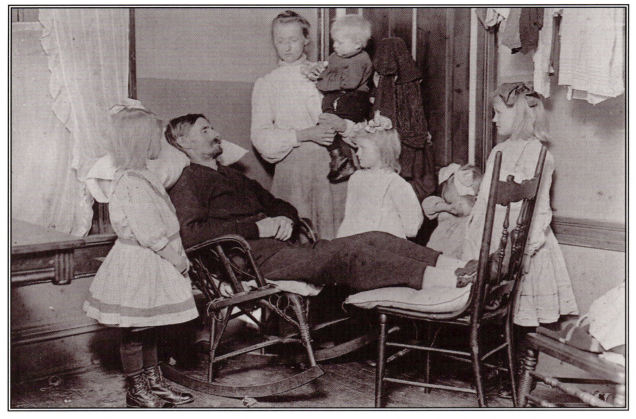

Washington, D.C. Crowded apartments sometimes made people sick and kept the sick from getting better. The father in this family suffers from tuberculosis.

Dirt, bugs, and crowding bred disease. Most families could hardly afford food, let alone a doctor when someone fell sick. Americans worried about the spread of disease in jam-packed buildings. New York finally passed a law requiring fire escapes, running water in each apartment, and a window in each room.

New York City. The Mauro family from Italy works at home piecing together feather decorations for hats.

Immigrants struggled. But they still dreamed of a golden future. In most families, everyone worked. Women and children rolled cigars, hemmed sleeves, or made brooms at home. They got paid by the piece. The Mauro family earned $2.25 a week stitching feathers for hats.

Somerville, Massachusetts. Two young factory workers take a break.

Some girls took jobs as servants. Many worked in factories. Small factories were so hot, dark, and cramped that they were called *sweat*shops. Workers sewed long hours, sometimes without a single day off. Factories posted signs: "If you don't come in on Sunday, don't come in on Monday."

New York City. A twelve-year-old boy in a city sweatshop

Boys worked on their own as well as in sweatshops. They shined shoes, sold newspapers, collected rags, delivered messages, or peddled peanuts.

New York City. Jewish immigrant girls protest child labor in 1909.

   Some immigrants demanded better wages and working conditions. They formed labor unions. Unions organized marches and held strikes.

   A terrible fire in New York City killed more than 140 factory workers in 1911. Most were young immigrant girls and women. After that, unions got more support from the public. States passed more laws against child labor.

Chicago. Children play in the street in a Polish neighborhood.

After work, children played tag on the roof or swam in fountains. Girls rolled hoops on the pavement while boys shot marbles.

It was fun to watch the comings and goings on the street. Immigrant neighborhoods hummed. Peddlers sang songs about their vegetables. Shopkeepers argued politics. Horses pulled streetcars. With a few pennies, a child could buy a sweet from a Greek candy shop or an orange drink from a Syrian carrying a jug on his shoulder.

Above: Schoolchildren at a public library in Gary, Indiana, hold signs showing their home countries. In 1910, almost 37 percent of people living in Gary and surrounding Lake County were born outside the United States.
Opposite page: Mexican immigrants in a Texas cotton field in 1919

AMERICA FOR AMERICANS

O! Close the gates of our nation, lock them firm and strong,
before this mob from Europe shall drag our colors down.
                                        —anti-immigrant verse, 1923

By law, children were supposed to go to school until they were 16. But many businesses posted "Boy Wanted" signs, and children went to work. Most families needed the wages of extra workers. Often only the youngest child studied full-time.

Children from a dozen countries sat next to each other in class. Public schools taught them to love their new home. Children saluted the flag. They played American games like baseball.

Parents had a lot to learn about their new country, too. Schools and companies offered evening classes for workers. Children usually leaped ahead of adults.

"We were embarrassed if our parents couldn't speak English," said one girl. When friends came over, she hid her father's Polish newspaper.

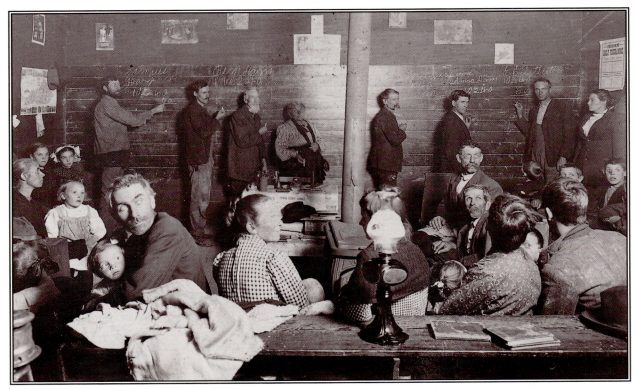

Kentucky. Grown-up and young immigrants take classes to learn English and other skills.

New York City. Immigrant children play on the rooftop of a settlement house.

Older immigrant groups offered loans and advice to new arrivals. They didn't want Americans to see everyone from their country as a greenhorn.

Rich Americans also felt a duty to help the poor. They opened settlement houses to help newcomers learn American ways. Part school and part neighborhood center, a settlement house usually had a playground, a library, a gym, and a kitchen. Volunteers gave classes in how to wash, dress, and cook American-style.

Many immigrants didn't want to change so much. They loved home as well as here. They felt they were losing their children. They started schools to keep their languages and religions alive.

New York City. Young Jewish immigrants study at a Hebrew School in an apartment building.

Washington, D.C. In 1925, thousands march in a rally of the Ku Klux Klan, a group that opposed immigration—mainly of Roman Catholics and Jews—to the United States.

Differences scared many Americans. Some schools, clubs, and neighborhoods turned away Jewish, Italian, or Japanese people. Dressed in white robes, hate groups paraded. They screamed that more established white Americans shouldn't mix with immigrants. They forgot that almost everyone in the United States started out as an immigrant—even the Pilgrims.

San Francisco. Chinese immigrants on the steps outside their home in about 1888

In 1882, the government passed a law to keep out Chinese workers. The United States was filling up its land and its jobs.

Next, inspections at the border grew tougher. Newcomers had to answer more questions. They had to pass a reading test. One boy crept under a table and whispered answers to his mother.

More laws, passed in the 1920s, slowed immigration from a wave to a trickle.

Children and grandchildren of immigrants grew up to be singers and scientists, painters and presidents. Their gifts made the United States rich. Bits of the old country crossed into the new. Soon Americans were eating Italian foods like pizza and using Yiddish words like *klutz*. And over time, every immigrant family became American in its own way.

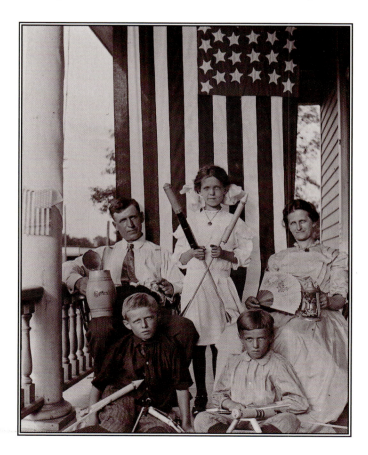

Saint Paul, Minnesota. For the Fourth of July in 1911, members of the Hedlund family celebrate their Danish, German, and Austrian roots— and their home in America.

Explore Your Country's Immigrant Past

The ancestors of everyone living in North America came from someplace else. Native American peoples first began traveling to North America from Asia thousands of years ago. Europeans came to start colonies on the East Coast and eventually forced Africans to come to America as slaves. Asians moved to western states and territories, helping to build America's railways. Immigrants continue to come to the United States every year.

Explore your country's immigrant history by choosing one of the options below:

A. Set aside time to interview your parents or grandparents or other older family members. How far back can you trace your family's history? Are you or any of your ancestors immigrants to this country? If so, where did you or your ancestors come from? When did you or your ancestors make the journey to America? Does your family own any items or photographs brought from your old home? Can any members of your family tell you what life was like for them in their old home? How is life in America different?

B. Contact a friend or neighbor who is willing to share his or her family history. Or ask your teacher or librarian for ideas on how to meet a recent immigrant to this country. Ask that person the same kinds of questions listed in option A above.

C. Research your town's or your city's immigrant past. What groups of people have lived on the lands where your town, neighborhood, or city is located? Who founded your town or city? What countries did those people come from? How long have people lived in your area? What brought them there? To trace your area's immigrant past, visit your local library or historical society. Ask to see any photographs showing old or recent immigrants to your town or city.

After conducting interviews or doing research, collect your findings and create a display showing your family's, friend's, or area's immigrant past.

NOTE TO TEACHERS AND ADULTS

For many children, the waves of immigration in the late 1800s and early 1900s may seem like part of a far-off past. But there are many ways to make this era and its people come alive. Along with helping children research family or community history, you can help them explore America's immigrant past in other ways. One way is for them to read more about the era. More books on the topic are listed on pages 44 through 46. Another way you can help young readers explore the past is to train them to study historical photographs. Historical photographs hold many clues about life in earlier times. Ask your children or students to look for the details and "read" all the information in each picture in this book. For example, many new immigrants in this book are pictured with American flags. Why would people coming from different countries want to be photographed with this patriotic symbol of America?

To encourage young readers to learn to read historical photographs, have them try these activities:

Mapping Immigrant Travels
On this book's front cover and on pages 1, 5, 8, and 9, you will find photographs of immigrants making the journey from their old homes to North America. Choose one of the immigrant children shown in the photos and try to imagine all the stops on that child's journey. Study both the photo and the text to answer these kinds of questions: Where was his or her old home? If the caption does not say, can you guess? How would this child have traveled to North America? What were typical stops along the way?

How would he or she have entered the United States? Draw a map showing the stops you imagine this immigrant would have made. For more details about an immigrant journey to the United States, read *Letters from Rifka*, a novel about a young girl from Russia.

Walking in an Immigrant's or Inspector's Shoes

The photographs on pages 10 through 17 show immigrants at different ports of entry to the United States in the early 1900s. Dress in costume as a new immigrant or as an inspector while a friend or classmate takes the other part. Work together to create a list of questions and answers for your characters. Then present your skit to family, friends, or classmates. Read the text—and the photographs—in this book for information and for details. To add to your presentation, read some of the books on pages 44 through 46. For an account of a boy's encounter with immigration inspectors, read *Dragonwings*, a novel set in San Francisco's Chinatown. Or take a look at *I Was Dreaming to Come to America*, a nonfiction book about immigrants arriving at Ellis Island.

Letters to Friends Back Home

Put yourself in the place of one of the immigrant children shown in this book and write a letter to your friends and family back home. Describe your new life in an immigrant neighborhood or on the frontier. How has your life changed since you left your old home? What do you miss most? What do you like most about your new life? What are your hopes for the future? To learn more about immigrant life in America, read *Chang's Paper Pony*, a story set in a California gold rush town, or *Brooklyn Doesn't Rhyme*, a novel set in an immigrant neighborhood in Brooklyn, New York.

Resources on Immigrants and Immigration

Blos, Joan. *Brooklyn Doesn't Rhyme.* New York: Charles Scribner's Sons, 1994. In this novel, sixth grader Rosey Sachs writes about her family and life in an immigrant neighborhood in Brooklyn, New York, after her new teacher explains that "knowing about your family will help you to know yourself."

Chermayeff, Ivan, et al. *Ellis Island: An Illustrated History of the Immigrant Experience.* New York: Macmillan Publishing Company, 1991. Chermayeff uses images and artifacts from the Ellis Island Museum in this book for adults.

Coan, Peter Morton. *Ellis Island Interviews: In Their Own Words.* New York: Facts On File, Inc., 1997. This book for adults includes short interviews with immigrants, many of whom came to this country when they were young.

Coerr, Eleanor. Pictures by Deborah Kogan Ray. *Chang's Paper Pony.* New York: Harper & Row, Publishers, 1988. In this book for beginning readers, Coerr tells the story of Chang, a young Chinese immigrant living in a California mining town in the mid-1800s.

Fisher, Leonard Everett. *Ellis Island: Gateway to the New World.* New York: Holiday House, 1986. Fisher documents the history of the United States' main immigration station with period photographs and first-person accounts.

Freedman, Russell. *Immigrant Kids.* New York: E.P. Dutton, 1980. Freedman tells the story of immigration around the turn of the last century with a special emphasis on children in eastern cities.

Heller, Linda. *The Castle on Hester Street*. Philadelphia: The Jewish Publication Society of America, 1982. Sitting down with their granddaughter, Julie, grandfather tells tall tales while grandmother tells the *real* story of their journey from Russia to America in this picture book.

Hesse, Karen. *Letters from Rifka*. New York: Henry Holt and Company, 1992. In letters she writes but cannot send to her cousin in Russia, a young Jewish girl tells the story of her roundabout journey to America, including a stay on Ellis Island.

Lawlor, Veronica. *I Was Dreaming to Come to America: Memories from the Ellis Island Oral History Project*. New York: Viking Press, 1995. Lawlor illustrates short quotations from immigrants who arrived at Ellis Island as children.

Leighton, Maxinne Rhea. *An Ellis Island Christmas*. New York: Puffin Books, 1992. It's Christmastime at the immigration station in this picture book.

Levinson, Riki. *Watch the Stars Come Out*. New York: Puffin Books, 1985. In this picture book, a grandmother tells the story of her mother, an immigrant who made the journey to America with her ten-year-old brother.

Littlefield, Holly. Illustrations by Mary O'Keefe Young. *Fire at the Triangle Factory*. Minneapolis, Minn.: Carolrhoda Books, Inc., 1996. In this beginning reader, two immigrant girls find that only friendship can save them when they are caught in a terrible fire at the Triangle Shirtwaist Factory in New York.

Maestro, Betsy. Illustrated by Susannah Ryan. *Coming to America: The Story of Immigration*. New York: Scholastic Inc., 1996. This nonfiction picture book surveys the history of American immigration, from 20,000 B.C. to modern times.

Morrow, Robert. *Immigration: Blessing or Burden?* Minneapolis, Minn.: Lerner Publications Company, 1997. Author Morrow presents the positive and negative sides of immigration in the United States.

Stanley, Diane. *Elena.* New York: Hyperion Books for Children, 1996. In this short novel, Stanley tells the story of a Mexican family moving to California to escape the Mexican Revolution of 1910 to 1920.

Yee, Paul. *Roses Sing on New Snow: A Delicious Tale.* New York: Macmillan, 1991. In this picture book, a young woman living in a West Coast Chinatown in the early 1900s creates a dish that blends Old and New World flavors.

Yep, Lawrence. *Dragonwings.* New York: Harper & Row, Publishers, 1975. A young Chinese boy joins his father in San Francisco's Chinatown in this novel set in 1903. Together, the boy and his father make a new life and dream of building an airplane.

Websites about Immigration
http://educate.si.edu/migrations/start.html
The Smithsonian Institution's Migrations in History Website looks at "what happens when people move, what they take with them, what they leave behind, and how they make their new place home."

http://www.bergen.org/AAST/Projects/Immigration/
Started as a project by a group of tenth-grade students, this Website offers information about the history of American immigration from the 1600s to the present.

New Words

greenhorn: a slang word for a newly arrived immigrant who knows little about local customs

immigrant: someone who comes to live in a new country on a permanent basis

settlement house: a community center, often located in an immigrant neighborhood, where people can meet, take classes, and get advice

strike: a temporary stopping of work by employees in order to force an employer to meet workers' demands

sweatshop: a workplace that is often overcrowded and unhealthy at which workers earn low wages

union: an organization in which workers join together to improve pay, benefits, and working conditions

Index

TIME LINE

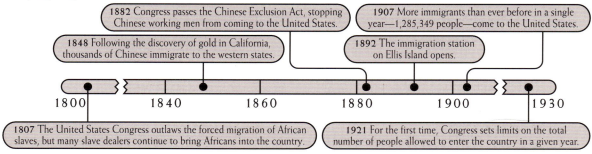

1882 Congress passes the Chinese Exclusion Act, stopping Chinese working men from coming to the United States.

1907 More immigrants than ever before in a single year—1,285,349 people—come to the United States.

1848 Following the discovery of gold in California, thousands of Chinese immigrate to the western states.

1892 The immigration station on Ellis Island opens.

1800 1840 1860 1880 1900 1930

1807 The United States Congress outlaws the forced migration of African slaves, but many slave dealers continue to bring Africans into the country.

1921 For the first time, Congress sets limits on the total number of people allowed to enter the country in a given year.

ABOUT THE AUTHOR

Sylvia Whitman lives with her husband and daughter in Orlando, Florida, and coordinates the writing center at Rollins College. She has degrees in folklore and mythology, American studies, and creative writing. Her publications for children include a half dozen history books.

"My ancestors came to North America a long time ago from England and Holland," she says. "My husband and daughter are both immigrants from Tunisia, an Arab country in North Africa. In Tunisia, most families have similar roots, so my husband is amazed at all the different kinds of people in the United States. In our house, we listen to Arabic and American music. We eat hamburgers and couscous, a North African pasta steamed over a stew of vegetables and lamb. It's fun to share our cultures."

ACKNOWLEDGMENTS

The publisher gratefully acknowledges the use of a quotation from Milton Meltzer, *Taking Root: Jewish Immigrants in America.* The photographs in this book are reproduced through the courtesy of: American Jewish Joint Distribution Committee, Historical Photo #29, front cover (colorized); Culver Pictures, back cover; National Geographic Society, National Park Service, Ellis Island National Monument, p. 1; Schlesinger Library, Radcliffe College, p. 2; A. B. Wilse, Norsk Folkemuseum, p. 5; Brown Brothers, pp. 6, 9, 11; National Park Service, Ellis Island National Monument, pp. 7, 8, 14, 16, 19; National Park Service, Ellis Island National Monument, Augustus F. Sherman Collection, pp. 10, 17; The Photo Collection, Carpenter Center for the Visual Arts, Harvard University, p. 12; National Archives, p.13; California Historical Society, pp. 15 (FN-18240 VIP01807), 22 (FN-02357), 38 (FN-22938); State Historical Society of Wisconsin, Dahl Collection, p. 18; Library of Congress, pp. 20 (LC-USZ62-23754), 21 (LCD401-12683), 27 (LC-H5-2709), 29 (LC-USZ62-10109), 30 (LC-USZ62-22198), 34 (LC-USZ62-8669), 37 (LC-F81-36635); Minnesota Historical Society, p. 23 (Photo by Ingersoll), 39 (Photo by Joseph Paulicek); Courtesy George Eastman House, pp. 24, 25, 26; Corbis/Bettmann, p. 28; Chicago Historical Society (Call #ICHI-20287; DN-000729), p. 31; Calumet Regional Archives, Indiana University Northwest, p. 32; Corbis/Bettmann-UPI, p. 33; University Settlement Archives, p. 35; Museum of the City of New York, p. 36.